Back Ground Check For Women

by
John F. Williams

Bloomington, IN  Milton Keynes, UK

authorHOUSE®

AuthorHouse™
1663 Liberty Drive, Suite 200
Bloomington, IN 47403
www.authorhouse.com
Phone: 1-800-839-8640

First published by AuthorHouse   5/19/2008

ISBN: 978-1-4343-0419-3 (sc)

Printed in the United States of America
Bloomington, Indiana

This book is printed on acid-free paper.

Background Check For Women

Some men don't understand women or what they want out of life with a man! Some women want their man to take them out to dinner or for a walk in the park. Sometimes they want to be alone with the love of their life! I have known many women during my life, and most women want the same thing out of life with a man! Some women want material things from a man. When you can't give a woman material things, it becomes a problem for her and for you. Some want a man that they can tell what they want and get what they ask for. If you can't do things for her, it sometimes causes a problem between the two of you. When women go out looking for a man, most of them are looking for a man who is smart and very articulate. Some women look at the way a man is dressed and they don't care how he talks as long as he has plenty of money. Overall, most women are looking for a man who treats them nicely, who is loving, who says sweet things, and who tells her how much he loves her and how she means so much to him. She wants to hear that she is the love of his life!

Some women don't want a short man, and others don't want a tall man or a fat man. If she is tall, she probably will not be interested in a short man. It doesn't matter to some women as long as he is smart and respectful. Someone who is perfectly productive is what women want out of men most of all! Some just want a man just to say they have a man. It doesn't even matter if he belongs to someone else or not! I, as a man, have been around woman talking about men, saying what they want from a man, saying what they want out of life. I have been with a lot of women in my life, and many women are just too much alike, but in different ways. Some women like going out to the clubs to enjoy the night life. Some like going to hear the orchestra. Going to the theater is what some women like to do, and others enjoy going out to dinner on the weekend. There are many things that women are different about when it comes to being happy with their man and their life. A man has got to sacrifice some of the things he likes to do in order to make his woman happy. It doesn't take that much to make a woman happy and secure by doing most of the things she wants to do in life! For those women who say they can't find a good man or that there are not any good men left, that's simply not true. There are plenty of good men out in the world. You just have to know who you are looking for. For women who are in search of a good man, you must first realize that you may never meet a man to fit your exact expectations. Be careful how you talk to a man and what you tell him you want from him. He may shy away or turn away from you. It's not so much what you said to him but how you said it to him. Where and how you meet a man can sometimes affect your relationship with a man! I understand that some women don't want a man who talks all of the time and that some women like a man to talk a lot so that they don't get board with the relationship. As a man, you must have a feel for a woman. If you can't find that feel for her, you may just be wasting her time and yours too! Some women like a man to invite them over for dinner at his house or apartment or wherever he may be living at the time. You have to take it slowly with some women when you first meet them. You don't want to pressure her about sex. Just work your way into it; it will come if she cares about you. After you have been with her for a while, she will feel comfortable.

Once she thinks you are this way, a man suppose to be with her and doing things with her taking her out dancing or to church. Just doing things that she like, she may not think much about her feelings toward you, she is being happy with you. I have heard woman say I don't love him but he's so nice to me. The comfort you can provide her means a lot to her. A woman likes her friends to make her laugh sometimes, and so you need to do these things sometimes with her because she will be quick to say she is bored with you. She may care about you but get bored sometimes. Just call her on the job and say "I love you." It's the small things that make them happy because when you get off the phone, they're going to tell their friends what you said that to them. Meeting a good woman can be difficult for some men because they don't know what to say. Conversation is very important to women. Being able to hold a conversation with a woman will cause her to take an interest in you and what you are saying.

Some women don't want to see a man if he doesn't have on name brand clothes or shoes. Some men don't buy name-brand clothes. Some don't know the difference between those who have on name-brand clothing and those who don't.

One man may drive an expensive car but not wear expensive clothes. You cannot look on the outside and see what you are looking for in a man. You need to see on the inside to see what he really looks like for yourself.

If you have a conversation with two men, you'll find out neither one of them may be the one. However, if you continue to look on the inside, you will soon find the one (if you aren't looking too far away from you). You can only look so far. You cannot look for a Rolls Royce if you are a Chevrolet. You cannot look for a mansion if you are a condo. This type of relationship is an uneven combination. In other words, look for compatibility. Sometimes this is what happens to most of the women who are looking for love. They are looking in the wrong places for love and comfort. Balance out your commonalities. If education is the most important quality you're looking for in a relationship, then both of you should be equally educated. It's not good for a woman to have a man who cannot afford to meet her needs because her standards will not be met.

This rule may be different for a man because he feels that he is supposed to provide for his woman and meet her needs. It doesn't have to be an equal balance for him as much as it must be for a woman! Today it's more common for couples to be equally suited. I don't think there are many couples who are married who have unbalanced incomes. Most of them are balancing out each other!

Your demeanor has a lot to do with the kind of man you want. I think when a man and a woman first meet they should talk about what they both are looking for in a friend. Then go from there and stay with what it is that brought you together. When the relationship takes a different turn, you should stop and talk about the progress. Discuss any problems when they first occur so that they can be dealt with. Women, don't be afraid to tell a man how you feel. However, when you first meet him, don't tell him you have lost hope in having a relationship. One of the main problems with women is that they have lost hope. When hope is lost, you may leap into something that is not good for you.

The first thing you do when you are looking for that special someone is see if they are a caring person. If you don't follow along some of these lines, then you may not find what you are looking for in a man. You just may find out that you don't like his table manners when you are out for dinner. It is not always going to be the way you would like it to be. The little things do not matter as long as the big ones are in place for you. You can work on the little things. Women usually have respect for their man. When you give respect, you will always get it. You can speak to a man in the polite way and he will give you respect. It's the way you speak to a man. He will give you the respect you gave him. Sometimes you don't want to be bothered. If you speak disrespectfully, then he will disrespect you.

Don't be rude when a man speaks to you or tries to come on to you. Just say "I'm sorry" or "No, thanks" or "I'm married." Smile when you say things like that to a man. You don't want to give him the wrong impression. If you are married, you can say "I am married. Thanks anyway!"

If you are single, don't fall for the first man who gives you a good look and a smiling face. He may not be good for you! Check him out like you would check out someone who is applying for credit. You are going on his credibility. Ask him to see his driver's license. By doing this, you can verify his name and his address. If he doesn't want to share this information with you, then continue to talk with him casually. Let him know that you enjoyed talking with him and get up from where you are and move on.

When he asks for your number, don't give it to him. Just say "I can't do that because it won'tl be good if I do that." If he offers you his number, just say "I rather not have it at this time, but it was nice talking with you. Maybe some other time." Then let the talk be over, and if he offers to walk you to your car, just say "That won't be good for me." If he continues to ask you, just say :I am not going to walk out of this place with you." If he asks why, you tell him that he is getting too personal. Now, when you leave him, you don't want to see him anymore. If you go some place again and see him, turn around and leave the place unless you are with some friends or with a male friend. He may have been everything on the outside, but the long talk with him wasn't what you were looking for in a man.

A long conversation with a man sometimes tells you about him. If you go beyond the conversation, then it may come after you are in a long relationship. There are a lot of things that a woman needs to look for in a relationship. If a man tells you that he has a woman who is just a friend or that he is married, he is not going to be true to you. I am not telling you to talk to him, but you can always say, "I don't care to be here having a conversation with you. You are married and your wife may come here at any time. She may not be looking for you but could be out with some of her friends, see us talking, and take it the wrong way. I don't want that to happen to you or to me. It would not be good for you, and I know it wouldn't be good for me." For you women out their looking for a man, you need to look for him in the right places. Sometimes you may find him in the church. This may be the kind of man you want. There are a lot of good men going to church. A man can be jealous, selfish, controlling, and many other things. How do you know it when you see it or hear it? Just be alert to what he says all of the time when you are having a conversation with him, because if he is some of these things, he is going to say something in that kind of way to you or about someone. He just may say that he don't want you going to the mall every week, and that's what you do after work. is go to the mall. Some men do not want his woman to stop any place after she get off from work. There are some times when you most likely will find some men who are jealous of their women, so you've got to watch out for that, because they have been watching the women out in a difference and they think most all women are that way. Once this man said to these men, "If you have plenty of money or some drugs, you can get any woman you want." I walked up about the time he was saying this to them. I stopped and told him that's not true. I asked him if I had plenty of money or drugs if I could have his mom. I said he should say that not all women are attracted to a lot of money or drugs. A lot of women don't want to get involved with men who deal with or who take drugs.

If you find a man who's thirty-five years of age, you need to check him out very well because most men that age are already married or have been married. If he has been married, you need to find out why he isn't with his wife. Ask him why he left her. It's hard to find a man you want if you don't do a background check on him. It's easier to find one if you do a background check on him. He is everywhere. He's at your work place, in your church, at the grocery store, the movie theater, at football games, and in many more places. The only way that you will find the man you are looking for is to do a background check on him. If you don't, it may be an easy relationship in the beginning relationship want be hard to get out off. if you do a back check for you or him. if you do not do a back grown check. Some women go for what they see, not for what it is. Handsome, tall, and good-looking are the qualities most women look for. He may be just good looking; that's all some woman want. They will think about what it is later when he starts to show his real self. Then she'll have to ask herself if she would have thought he was this way before dating him. What she should have done was a background check. Believe me, there are a lot of good men out there. You just have to know how find them.

Men are looking too, just like you, for a good woman. Sometimes it's the way you are dressed when you are out in public. When you are out, always look as good as you possibly can. Never go to the grocery store with hair rollers in unless you have something wrapped around your hair. Have the wrap tied in some kind of fashion on your head. If you don't know how go to use a wrap stylishly, then go to the salon and get them to teach you how to tie a beautiful wrap. When you go shopping at the mall, you can sometimes find good men at the mall. He could be there for you. You never know where your husband just may be for you. Just because a man doesn't have the look you want him to have doesn't mean he's not the man for you. He may be the perfect person you can go out on a date with because this man may be what you are looking for and you don't realize it. He may be the person you can be with when you are lonely at night or someone to talk to when you need that special one person to have a conversation with. Don't always look to far ahead, because he may slip away from you while you're looking ahead.

I know a little something about women, and I do know that some of them have goals that are very high. This is why they date a lot of men before they find the right one. But what happens with them is that they reach too high. The next thing that happens is a man has taken a woman's heart before she can think to do a background check on the man!

When a woman finds a man, she must find the man that she has something in common with; for example, the love of football, or basketball, or sitting at home watching movies on TV. There are many things to look for in a man if you want it to work out for you. In a relationship someone has to be the one with the managing mind. If you are in a relationship with a man, don't always assume that he is supposed to take care of the check. Offer to take care of the check sometimes and see what his response will be. If he lets you pay for the check, keep a close watch on him because he just may be looking for other things from you. He may tell you he wants to pay for the dinner this time and that maybe some other time you can take him out if you want. These days some women are making just as much money as their men. Some women make more than their men do. You can't think that men aren't watching that. Some men will think that they should pay all of the tabs when you go out on the town. Women, I am sorry, but some men don't think like that. Nowadays men are saying that women have just as much money as they do. Men talk about the women who want everything done for them. They call these women "gold diggers." A young man told his mom that if he has to drive his car and put gas in it, his girlfriend has to pay for the event they are going to!

Women, you must know that times have changed. If a woman and her boyfriend come to an agreement, especially when both of them are in college trying to support themselves, then that is fine. College women should pay for their food and college men should pay for theirs. If one of them doesn't have any money, then one of them could pay for both of them. You sure can learn a lot about a man in college. College gives you the time it takes to know the kind of man you want. It's not so much about what his parents have, because what his parents have is theirs. It can be somewhat of an advantage for you, and sometimes it can be a problem for you too. If his family is more financially successful than your family, this can cause confusion between the two of you. His family may not treat you like they should unless you come from a family that has finances like theirs. So, you young girls who are in college, watch out and do a background check on the young man that you may have your eyes on. I have never attended college, but I have been to a lot of colleges and have seen a lot of ladies on the wrong side of time. All I am saying is don't get on the wrong side of time because today is what's happening.

Being caught up in materialistic things is what happens to a lot of women. If a man speaks to you, don't just walk by like he didn't speak to you. Men don't like it when they speak to a woman and she doesn't speak back. If you don't want to speak, just smile and keep on walking. He will get it! If a man says "good morning" or "good evening" to you, you can simply say "same to you" and keep walking or doing whatever you are doing. If he wants to have a conversation and you are busy, just say you can't talk now. The wrong thing to do is to let someone hook you up with one of their friends. I have never told anybody to hook me up with their friend. It's not appropriate for someone to hook you up with their friend. Most of the time, it doesn't work out! Background checks are the best thing to do. If you decide to let your friend hook you up with someone, it doesn't matter what your friend may tell you about that person. If you do your background check, then you'll have all the information you need about the person. If you don't do a background check, you will have yourself to blame! For you to know it will work out, you need to know if you have something in common with each other. Both of you must have something in common for it to work out. When you meet a man, be yourself and no one else. It is very important for you to be true to yourself. When there is a problem between the two of you, he'll know where you stand.

Women, if you have a problem meeting the man of your life, it may be just you. Sometimes that can lead to something big for you. Some of you get upset with yourself and lose your self-esteem. Don't lose your self-esteem, because when you lose your self-esteem, it lowers your energy. That's when depression comes into your life, so you don't let these things happen in your life. Meeting a man depends on you and your self-esteem. Don't be too shy. Also, don't worry about things like your hair not being in place or if you have enough lipstick on, or if you have on too much perfume, or if your dress is suitable. Don't think about these things when you meet a man for your first time. Believe me, he is going to be too busy trying to see if he is correct for you. Some men don't seem to care about how they look when they meet a woman. This doesn't mean they don't care about themselves. When you go out looking for a man, go to the makeup shop and let them make up your face for you. It doesn't cost that much for you to stop by a merchant to get your face made up before going out for the evening. All of this may seem like too much to do when you are going out, but it is appropriate to do these things.

When you find the man of your dreams, don't be too demanding with him. Try to be agreeable and compromising with each other. One thing about most women is that they live their relationships with their family and friends. That's not good for your relationship with your partner. Tell your friends all of the good things about your man and keep all of the bad things to yourself. I think that it would make a better relationship for you and your man. Most women who are financially stable don't need someone to bring them anything. You need to make it clear to your man that you can get all of the things you want and need for yourself. However, it's different for other women who are not financially secure. So it's not so hard for a woman to check a man's background if she is interested in a man she has met.

You may meet that special someone at the service center or maybe at a clothing store. It doesn't matter where you meet him. Just be ready to do your background check at all times because you never know where he may be. Sometimes being alone out in a restaurant will get a man's attention. A bar or a nightclub is not the best place to be alone and trying to find a man. It's unsafe to be out at these places alone at night. Men think that you are something different, meaning that they may think you came to the bar or nightclub to talk or to meet someone. Bars and nightclubs are not the right place to be if you are looking for a serious relationship with a man. Most women who are out in the bars at night have been out in them most of the time and are looked at as call girls or prostitutes. Not all of them are, but most of them are. They are at the bar for something a little different than you would be at the bar for, so that could be a problem for a person like you. If you are a woman who has been divorced and who has children, the first thing you should do is tell the man that you are talking with how many kids you have and their ages. This is very important because some men don't want a woman if she has children. To other men, it doesn't matter if she has children or not.

It is very important for you and your kids to talk over you having met someone who may become a good friend. If one of them objects to you having a friend, then talk to that child about it and ask why he or she objects to you having a friend. It may be they have not gotten over being without their dad. In this case, you can't ignore what has been said to you, because he or she isn't going to be friendly to him. You can't make a child be something they don't want to be. The first thing for you to do is to let your kids meet him. See how he will introduce himself to them. Make sure you have checked him out around children other than his own. This is very important for you and the kids. See if he treats your kids just like they are his kids or if he acts like he doesn't want to be bothered with them. If you see any signs of this you certainly should call the relationship off. Don't ever let him stay at your house alone with the children while you are dating him because it could cause a problem if you have girls between the ages of twelve and fourteen. It can be unwise too with boys around that same age. So it would be best for you to go to your man's house until they say when he can stay with them. It wouldn't be right to let him stay all night when you aren't married. It is not respectful to you or the children. When you are in a relationship with a man, let your kids have a say in the relationship about the man because there just may be something that you can't see in him. Some kids aren't going to like anyone but their dad. You have to talk to them and tell them how lonely you are without a man in your life!

There are three things you need to do first. Please your kids. Second, please yourself. Third, please the man! What happens with women when they are in a relationship with a man is that they sometimes forget about the kids. They turn to the man just a little more than necessary. Because it's hard for some women to meet a man and still be who they really are, sometimes they lose the truth in themselves. This happens with them at an early age, usually in their teenage years. When they grow up as a young woman, their self-esteem is down. This is why it is very hard for some women to get the man of their choice. Men sometimes take all of a woman's heart, mind, and body. When that happens to them, it's hard for them to trust again. Some don't let that happen to them again. Her heart can continue to break, but she won't let that control her mind.

Most women look for love, not materialist things out of a man, because in today's world, it's not a problem with them. They can get that all by themselves. When you get a man, don't let him use your body in a way that makes him think it all belongs to him. It's your body and not his. You just let him be connected with it sometimes. Don't stop going out on your own or with your friends. You want to stay familiar with the way of meeting men. If something happens with this man, you won't be so devastated over the breakup. You don't want to be untrue to him, but be involved with other men at least once a week. Just talking to another man and still being dedicated to your friend will help you if the relationship doesn't last. When you are out in the clubs, check men out on how they pay for their drinks. Some men pay with their credit card; others pay with cash. How do you determine the difference in the two men? One may have on a suit and the other may have on jeans. This is not going to help you determine the difference between the two men. By having a conversation with both men, you will be able to determine the difference between the two. You can't learn or know a man the first time you meet him, but you can have a feel for what kind of man he may be.

Meeting a man is not hard to do. The problem is getting the one for you. He may be most women's dream but not your dream. You should go after the man you see, not what anyone else says about a man. You are the one who has to spend time with this man. Your feelings are what count in the relationship. Spending time with this man and getting to know him, along with a background check, keeps your heart out of everything. After the background check, it's up to you if he checks out the way you want a man to check out! He may not check out for another woman, but he may check out for you. If all women do this with men, they will most likely find out that a relationship with this man may work out. Never let a man get too close in your mind. This is what most smart men try to do when they first meet a woman. Don't let him get too close. Just let him get close enough for him to think he is all the way into your heart and mind.

Some men only want to get in a woman's heart and mind without giving their heart and mind to the woman. If you do allow this to happen, you will not have any control of your heart and mind, because he will have it.

Don't let a man know your income unless you have the kind of job that allows most anyone to know your yearly income. Some things you just don't tell other people. It takes years before you really know a man. Then sometimes you may go a lifetime and not really know him. It doesn't mean that you believe everything that he tells you but that it's the trust you have in him that makes you believe him. Women who are lonely should find something to occupy their minds, like reading a book to keep from being depressed. Visit the mall or visit some of your friends. Whatever you do, let it be productive. Men can tell by the way you talk if you are interested in his conversation. He will continue to talk to you if you are interested and interesting. He will find something to talk to you about. It doesn't take a wise man long to figure out if you are interested in him. He will soon move away from you and find another woman to talk to if you are not interested. Most of the time it's you he wants to talk to, but you didn't give him that impression. Sometimes you will meet a man who is different from other men. He will have a different attitude toward you and may have been turned away from most of the women he has been trying to talk to. When you meet someone, always keep him thinking how sure you are of yourself with conversation. Most men are afraid to talk to a woman if they think she is very intelligent. She may be too beautiful for them. There are a lot of things about women that can turn a man off from pursuing her. So you must know how to meet with men when you are out looking for one. Women aren't going to find a man by sitting around feeling down about themselves. Get out and meet men. When you meet men, don't be all uptight with them. Be open about yourself. Tell them where you are coming from and where you want to go in life. When you get a good man, treat him like you care about him. Getting him and keeping him is what you have to do. Don't let your love get old. Keep it burning. Don't let the flame go out, because it will be hard to get the fire back. If you stay on your level, it's not going to be hard for you to find the man you are looking for.

Sometimes a man can see you long before you see him because he has been looking longer. Some women go on the internet looking for a man. I think that's the wrong way to look for a man who you may want to spend the rest of your life with. If you do a background check, it could be okay to try having a relationship, but the best way to meet a man is face to face because you can see what you are getting into. This is why most marriages don't work out the way women want them to. It is very important to do a background check for yourself. If you meet someone out and don't want to be bothered, you can always act pressed for time. If you aren't really pressed for time, you may want to hold a conversation with him. If this man doesn't look like he fits your needs, then that would be a good enough reason not to converse with him. It was his look that wasn't satisfactory enough for you. It didn't matter to you what he was driving. It's not good to get someone that you can't stand to look at or be around.

For some women, materialistic things can get you into something that's hard for you to get out of. So don't take those kinds of chances with men. It can be devastating for you! It's always easy to meet a man, but meeting the man for you and your needs can be hard or easy. Just grabbing someone that looks like a man with a man's features and talks like a man doesn't make him a man. A man who is respectful toward a woman can present himself in a manner such as opening doors for you, taking you out to dinner, and being respectful to your family and friends. When you meet a man with some of these qualities, then he may be the man for you—if you do a background check on him! A man will give his woman the right to most all of the decision-making and vacation-planning for the family, which ever it may be. If you meet a man, he will ask you if you would like to go to the beach or on a weekend stay in the mountains or just take you to a place of your choice for the weekend. This is some of the relationship things that a man will do for a woman who means something to him. When you meet a respectful man and you have children, he will ask you to let him take the kids to a park or to a movie on the weekend or to a football game. If they are small children or teenage children, then he may ask them if they want to go to a professional game on the weekend with the both of you. This sometimes will tell you something about this man. Most respectful men will do these things with you and your kids. If a man never asks to take you and your kids to a park or to some kind of sporting event on the weekend, then this man may not be the man for you and your kids. You should do a background check on the man that you are planning to spend your life with and your kids!

Don't let a man just tell you about himself without doing a background check on him. It's very important for you and your children or for you if you don't have any kids. For you women who are in college, it is very important for you to do a background check on the young man that you are thinking about getting involved with because he could be a young man whose parents have done everything for him. He will be thinking that you are supposed to do for him like his parents have. A lot of women will say all of the good men are taken, but that's not true. If you look in different places, you may find a good man quicker than you think. You may say, Where is that? Change the area you have been looking. It's the kind of man you are looking for also. If you are looking for a man that goes to church, then you must look for him in church. If you like a man that likes the night life, you must look for him in some of your night clubs or at some of the exclusive restaurants in your city. These are some of the places you might look for your companion. A lot of relationships aren't compatible. Sometimes things appear not to go well with you in a relationship. So it is very important that if your man likes sports, you like some kinds of sports in order to have fun in this relationship. During basketball and football season, your man is going to spend a lot of time watching these games on television. While he's watching these games on television, you are going to get bored and make it uncomfortable for him if you don't like sports. Most women these days like sports. Most women born in the early '40s may not know the game, but know when there is a touchdown or when the team scores two points. This is why a background check should be done on the man you are looking to have a relationship with. You should be happy in your relationship with him, and it should be the same for him too. When you find the man of your life, ask him if he would like to go shopping with you. If not, go alone unless you don't like going alone. This is very important in your relationship because most men don't like going shopping with their woman. If he doesn't want to go shopping with you, just say something sweet to him to get him to go. Say something he likes to hear from you; for example, "We are going to make love when we get back from shopping." Now, that is something that will make him happy. He will smile and go shopping with you. When you get back home, keep your promise to him.

Some women want too much from a man. When dating him, take him out sometimes. A man will love that from you because he wants to think you are not a gold digger. Most men think of women these days as gold diggers. Let him know that you are a woman who doesn't need him for support because you support yourself. You need a man for comfort. You need someone to love you and say sweet things to you. Mean what you say, and if he can't do these things for you, you don't need him.

A man and a woman should sign a prenuptial agreement because what you have is yours. There are not too many men who are going to try to take from you what's not theirs. Men think women are gold diggers even if they are making one hundred thousand dollars a year. A woman will still want him to pay all the checks for her. This can be bad for a man if he is not making but sixty thousand a year. She should share some of the checks sometimes if he is the man she would like to have in her life. I was listening to the radio one morning, and this woman had gone out on a date with this guy. They were asked if they wanted wine for dinner and the man said that he didn't drink wine but that if she wanted wine with her dinner, it was okay with him. I think that she said she didn't go out with him anymore. Some people don't drink wine for dinner at home or when they go out. I didn't think that was sophisticated for her to stop dating him because he doesn't drink wine. Somewhere along the way, she didn't do her background check. This is why it's important to do a background check.

Women sometimes overlook the man in life by looking above their expectations or below their expectations. The reason for this is because they don't do the background check. It can be humiliating for women. As women grow older, they get set in their own ways in life, and it may be hard for you to find someone to meet your standards. The only thing for sure is that you will need to change some of your ways if you want to find a man. Some women's lives are golden because they don't worry about having a man in their life. Women don't care about a man being with them. Women who are concerned about having a man in their lives are usually your low-income women. All women want to be married at some point in time in their lives to see what married life is all about.

Some women don't like to hear other women talk about what they did with their husband or where they have been on the weekend or what restaurant they went to. They feel pressured. If a man isn't talking about getting married in six months, then you may consider asking him if it is in this relationship plan for you, because it's been going on too long. If you are wanting to get married and have kids or just want to be married to this man, then give him an ultimatum about what you want out of life. If he loves you, he will meet the ultimatum you give him. If it isn't love, he will try to suggest another way to you because he's not ready for this with you. You as a woman must think about all of these things when you get into a relationship with a man. This is another reason why you must do a background check on a man before you get involved with him.

It's easy for a woman in college to do background check on the man she is interested in, because she is there with him on campus every day. She will get to know him the way she should get to know him. At the same time, doing a background check on him and keeping your heart out of the relationship until you get all of your information back will help. If he checks out the way you want him to check out, go with your heart and not your mind. Keep your mind open about him until he tells you he wants to spend the rest of his life with you. Then ask him, "How are we going to do that?" If he says you'll do it by getting married, if you are ready, then say yes. When you aren't with him, you should trust him because of your relationship with each other. These are some of the things you must do in a relationship with a man. Do you know his parents' background? Do you want to go on his parents' background or just his background? If you want to know something about his parents, then it's okay, but you aren't getting involved with them. It's him you are getting involved with.

When you are trying to meet a man, don't let him know that you are lonely for someone to love you. When you first meet a man, don't let him be all into you, such as touching you inappropriately. You must be attentive to all of these things. Don't fall down so low that he thinks he can touch you anytime he wants to. This is your life that you are dealing with. This is your heart and mind. When your heart and mind are gone, you don't have anything to protect the body. This is why they say a mind is a terrible thing to waste. Don't let this happen to you. Don't let someone treat your body inappropriately. Don't let him have all of your mind and body until he has made a commitment to you. Giving him your heart and mind is an incredible thing. Always remember to keep away the thing that makes him feel good; whatever it may be, as long as it is the thing that make's him happy. By doing these things, he will do most anything to be happy with you. He may want your heart and mind too. He can't have it all. However, it's not good for you to let him have all of that. What are you going to have left? If he has your heart and mind, what can you do for other people without a mind? Your heart you love with and the mind you think with. If you have kids, how are you going to love and help them? Be careful not to let a man use you up. I hear people saying "he used her up." No, he didn't use you; you used yourself up. He can only do what you let him do. So get over it. This is why these things happen, and when they do happen, you want to blame it on the man. Blame yourself. Your impulsive thinking can get you into trouble. You must have dignity. When you have your dignity, not only do you respect yourself, but others will respect you too.

When you are out, whether it's day or night, you should always be dressed appropriately. If you want to find the right man, always present yourself in the right manner. Men are always out, and you never know where Mr. Right is going to be. Be on guard for him because he just may be next door. He could be anyone, anywhere. Always keep your car washed because that could be a stump in your way. Your car can say a lot about you, such as, Is your house clean? Having a dirty car could give the wrong impression about you. Most of the time, when a woman's car is dirty, her house is the same way. Always keep your house and car clean if it's possible for you, especially when you are out man-hunting. When you are out looking for that special someone, think about whether he is going to be a person that you can like. Think whether or not you will like your life with this person. If you aren't looking for someone to take up much of your time, then it will be okay.

When you find a man, don't expect for him to do all of the things that you want and none of the things he wants to do. You should be willing to do the things he wants to do too. Some men don't care about those things. This is why a background check should be done when you are looking for your special love. If you are going to buy something new for yourself or for your house, you should talk it over with him and see how he reacts. If some of these things aren't done, then the relationship will not work. Communication between the two of you is critical. If communication is a problem, there will always be some kind of misunderstanding in the relationship and all of this will lead to a breakup or divorce. The key to a good, solid relationship is having a clear understanding between the two of you. If that isn't there, then you will be unsatisfied with one another. It is important for the both of you to have an understanding in your relationship.

A prenuptial agreement is the way you both can agree on what both of you have brought into the relationship. I think both of you should start with what you had when you met, your love for each other and what you have when you all met is yours and what he had is his own. Then start from there because you can help each other. Maybe one of you hasn't had the chance to create financial success. For example, if he has a prosperous business and is in the need for some capital, it would be okay for you to help him and vice versa. My advice would be for you to get everything on paper, signatures, attorney, and all. What you create together will belong to the both of you. You can create a business partnership.

Women, when you find a man and you begin dating, keep a distance between you at all times. Men try to take over when you don't keep a distance from him. By letting him take over your body, you lose control. Don't let him have all of yourself. Make him wait on it because this is the most important thing your have. Make sure you have done your background check. Don't let your guard down during the dating time of your relationship with him. Most women let a man know all about them after they have been dating for a week or more. This is when you lose respect from the man. I know that in today's world, there are different kinds of sex. This isn't the kind of sex that is supposed to be happening. According to the dictionary, having sex is when a man takes his penis and enters into the vagina. All of the other ways are not in my dictionary. Oral sex is a new way of having sex. Back in the late '50s and '60s, you didn't hear about oral sex. If you heard about it, then most men in those days didn't want you around them. At least that's the way it was with black men. I can't speak about other races of people. What I am saying to women is don't do any of these things with your friend when you meet him. I hear some of the teens saying that they didn't have sex with a young man; they just had oral sex with him. They don't see oral sex as having sex. For a young woman to start her life off with oral sex. Don't destroy your young age with this kind of sex, because you don't know where else this young man has been before he started dating you. These are the things that satisfy men, not you. If this is the way he wants you to satisfy him, then you must tell him you aren't that kind of woman, but you can't stop him from getting what he wants, and he can get it elsewhere. He will respect you more for not doing it with him. This is how you get respect from men. Don't think that a young man isn't going to tell his friend what you did with him. I know this is what they do in today's world, but let it be with someone you are married to.

When it comes to getting a man, you must always give and demand respect from men. Don't receive all of the gifts that he offers you. Some men think by offering you gifts, they can influence you to do the things they want you to do. It's not good to receive everything that he has to offer you. Jewelry is a way to a woman's heart. Most men will try to impress you with jewelry. Some men want to impress you by bragging about what they have given you. They are trying to impress others. There are many ways that men will come after you when trying to date you. If you are a materialistic woman, this is how he will get your mind. Don't be a gold digger, but be a woman with high standards for yourself.

It is good to know his yearly income because you may have feelings for this man but his income isn't what you need for it to be. Some women will say they don't mind dating a man who makes less money than they do so long as he is willing to treat a woman with love and respect. That's just great if you aren't going to pressure him later on in the relationship about money. This is why I say to women you need to find men who are on your income level and who believes in the same religion. Find a man who's smart and respectful to you and who has a good sense of humor. If you date a man with a different religious preference, it's not going to work, because you have different beliefs.

Women, when you get the man in your life, try to keep the fire burning in the relationship. Sometimes when they get a man in a relationship, some women start letting themselves go. Don't let the real you leave the relationship. Sometimes this is what causes men to go outside the marriage or the relationship. Men are like children. They like their wife or girlfriend to pamper them. When you do these things to him, then you will see the difference in him. I am saying this to women because men like their women to take charge most of the time. If you don't do these things with your man, other women outside the relationship will do these things with him. This is why it's very important to keep your man happy at all times. If you don't have sex when you aren't feeling like having sex with him, some men can understand. However, most men will not understand. If he can go out for a couple of hours and get his needs met and come back home, then he will. If your job is causing you not to want to please your man at home, then you may think about changing jobs because it's causing a problem in your marriage. Some men will go along with you because they don't want to lose the marriage. This is something I thought some women needed to know about men. Women, up front, you need to let men know that you are out to find a man to have a relationship with. If you have children, you need to let them know that to love you means to love your children. Make sure you tell him what you want from the relationship. Today's world is different with men because they see women doing things to other men and they are afraid to get serious with someone special. Be special to him at all times when you are with him so that he won't think that you are just like the other women he's been with. Some men will think that all women are the same way. For about seven years, I thought that all women were the same until I met a special woman. She made me feel different about women. Sometimes it has a lot to do with the way you were treated in your last relationship. You can't think the same way about all men you meet in your life.

In a relationship someone will be humiliated if you aren't being true to each other. It doesn't mean that one of you will have to be with another person. It can be about someone saying things. You may say something small and it comes across as something big to your other half. We shouldn't think that anything we say is small. It may seem small to you but huge to someone else. Sometimes things don't always go the way we plan. If it continues to be unpredictable, that's when the distrust comes into play with the couple. When you are planning to take your friend or wife out, you shouldn't promise, because sometimes they will say "you promised me" and that can be humiliating. I say don't make promises to anyone, because you may not be able to keep them.

Sometimes, women, you will get your friend or your husband to promise things. When and if he cannot keep his promise, you will use it against him. I don't think that you should do that to your friend or husband because you were the one who talked him into promising you in the first place. If he tells you himself, then it may be a problem with you. If he promises you, he most likely will do what he has promised. For example, maybe he promises you he will be there on time to take you out to dinner or to a movie. If he doesn't keep his promise, then you can complain to him about it. I know that sometimes men are going to tell you things with the intention of doing them, but sometimes things come up. The difference between a man and a woman is that when women tell their men something, they are most likely to do it. It doesn't make any difference what comes up. Whatever you are doing, you are going to manage to do what you said you were going to do, even if you may not care that much for him. This is natural for women. Integrity means a great deal to women. Sometimes you are too possessive with men and that can make a difference in your relationship. Some of you aren't possessive enough. You let your man take charge of your relationship. Some men want you to take charge of the relationship. Some women need to know some of these things about men when involved in a relationship.

Don't expect things from him. If he doesn't do some of the things you want him to do, you have to tell him. Some men don't want their friends to tell them where to go or when they can go. Some men are living in the past and can't move forward. Once again, this is why you need to do a background check on the man you are trying to date before you get too involved in a relationship. Some women look for things in a relationship beyond their needs. They should be looking for important things in their lives to happen. Most women look for materialist things from a man. Instead of looking for a man to do things for her, a woman should be looking for a man that she can do things together with in a relationship. Today it is not all about you. It's about the both you being together in a relationship. Some will say if a man can't do for them, they don't want to have anything to do with him. That's not the way a relationship is supposed to be. Once women figure that out, they will come to see their relationship will be better.

Some women want a man to come into their lives to pay their mortgage and car payment. Well, there aren't many men like that today,, unless he is someone who's making two or three hundred thousand dollars a year, and there are not that many available men out there making that much money a year unless they are a rap artist, the president of a company, or a professional ballplayer. Sometimes it will work, but not too often. I am not saying that this is impossible, because it can happen. I can say that it doesn't happen too often—maybe one out of a thousand. For instance, Labron James has a woman that he dated in high school. There are not too many women who can get a man with that kind of background in today's world. All women are looking for that kind of man. It doesn't happen that way too many times in life.

Every woman is looking for that special kind of man who can take care of her, but there are not that many men around with that kind of financial success. There may be more European men with that kind of financial success, but not with African American men. There are just a few black men who can do all of the things a woman wants, because black men don't have the jobs that the European men have. European men won't give African American men the jobs they deserve. They will give jobs to the African-American women before they give them to the African American men. This is how it is in America today. So, if you are a black woman, don't ask what the black man can do for you these days. You should be asking what you can do for him. This is a together world today. It's not a one-way relationship anymore. It's a two-way relationship. Don't go out looking for a man to take care of your bills. Look for a man who is respectful to you.

I heard my son tell my wife that he wasn't going to pick up his girl unless she was going to put the gas in his car because he had the car. She is supposed to put the gas in if she wants to go out. This is how some young men are today. Women, you must think of the men you are trying to have in your life. It's not all about you, because men aren't going for that today. It's a new world out there. Things in the past can't be brought back. The past is in the past. Some women want a man to take them out to expensive restaurants and help them with their finances too. This is not going to happen with most men in today's world. You may find some men who are willing to help with all of these things. You have to wonder though, what is going to be behind all of this? Some men give you their money and think that they own a part of you. This is why most men today want a prenuptial agreement when they get married because they think women are marrying them for their financial status. This may be for his and her best interest. Women should always do a background check on a man that she is thinking about spending the rest of her life with.

We all know today if you can find a couple that's been married more than twenty-five years they have been by each other's side. They went into the marriage to make each other happy by loving and caring for each other. Sometimes when you are in a relationship you have to give a little to make the relationship work. If neither one of you is willing to give in a little, it isn't going to work.

Who is the main attraction in the relationship? Is the woman the main attraction in the relationship? A woman who's in a relationship will work with a man. She is willing to go a mile for him when he is only willing to go a yard for her. Women will forgive five times more then a man will. It doesn't make any difference what the situation is. This is just the way men are. So, women, don't get caught up in difficult situations with your man. Don't try to make him understand, because it's his integrity and pride that will make him not forgive you. His pride won't let him forgive you for whatever reason. It is his egotistic mind that tells him not to forgive you. His heart wants to forgive you for the situation, but his mind will not let him. What I am trying to tell you is let him do the forgiving, not you, if you want the relationship to work. Men have had their way with woman ever since back in the days of King David. Today is the new millennium. So, you women out their today, stand up for liberty. I am not saying that women should not forgive. I am saying that you are usually the one doing all of the forgiving and that sometimes it needs to be accepted from men just as well as from women.

Women, you need to study men before you get into a relationship with a man, because men are jealous people. It doesn't make any difference what kind of man he is and what his status is. It doesn't make any difference if he is liberal. A man who has integrity will not be this way with a woman, because he will not give her any reason to say he's being selfish. He will listen to what she has to say.

There was a man that I knew who liked to look at women with big butts, and his woman didn't like him to look at other women with big butts. She had a big butt, so what she did was go out and bought some shorts that were very short. She wore them. Well, it didn't stop him from looking at other women with big butts. She divorced him and wanted him to pay for the shorts that she had bought. The judge told her it was her doing, not him, because she saw that he didn't have any respect for her or any other woman. She told the man that he was disrespectful and dismissed the case. This woman was upsetting to the judge because she settled for a man who had no respect for women. This is what some men will do to you when they get into your heart. When they get into your heart, they get your mind. Then you have nothing left for yourself but a body for him to do whatever he wants with. Sometimes, depending on the woman, this can lead to prostitution. You don't have the mindset to not do these things for him, because he is telling you that if you don't do these things, you don't love him. This is what I know, not what I think. Someone told me this because he once had control over a woman's mind by getting into her heart. It can be easy to do with a woman once you get her heart! The mind will soon follow the heart because this is what the heart is telling the mind. Once you lose your mind, you have nothing to control the other parts of your body. All the heart does is keep the blood flowing, and it's up to your mind to keep everything else in good condition. So I say to young women, don't let your heart interfere with your mind. A mind is not to be wasted, because you do everything with your mind. It is very important to do a background check on the man you are getting involved with. It doesn't take as long to do a background check as it does to get away from misery.

Women, if you aren't checking up on men when you are out there, you will get something that you don't want. When you first met this man, you thought that there was no other man like him until you moved further on into the relationship. Now you are trying to find a way out of the relationship, but you may have let it get too far. Sometimes, before you get into a relationship, you need to see how a man will talk. You can play it by ear, meaning listening to what he says to you and the way he says it to you. If you don't like what you hear, this would be a good time to let the relationship cease.

My attorney would tell me "we are going to play this by ear," meaning we weren't going to make our move until we hear from the other party. Play it cool and listen to your friend to see what he is all about. The only way for you to learn is by listening to what he has to say to you at all times when you are with him. If you are on the phone with him, always listen. It just may be something that he said to you that you wanted to hear from him. It can happen anywhere and anytime, so this is why it's very important for you to listen to what he has to tell you. Women, you must know your man. If you don't know the man in your life, it will not be a happy life for you because you will always be trying to get to know him. Some women never get to know their man. They try to make him into something or someone else. This will never work. If some of you women are doing this, you will be trying to change men in all of your relationships.

The most difficult situation in any relationship is when women try to be difficult about having sex with their man. This attitude can send your man shopping for it in other places. Women aren't like men when it comes to sex. When you aren't having sex with your man, this is what you are doing. You are sending him out there to get it from someone else. Some men won't do that to you because they don't want to lose you because of sex problems. It doesn't need to be because of sex. These are some of the things that some women need to know about their relationship with their man. Some of you women out there are doing these things with your man, and you need to stop and take back over your relationship. Stop saying he is sleeping with another woman. You know you ran him out to do these things with another woman. This wasn't his doing; it was your doing. You didn't want to give him the sex he needed from you. These are some of the things that happen in a relationship.

It isn't always about you in the relationship. Stop trying to make your man happy the wrong way, such as being too demanding of him. Sometimes you should ask him what he wants to do or where he wants to go for the weekend. Tell him to take control of all of your weekend plans. If he just chooses to stay at home, then that's what you do with him without complaining. Some men aren't going to do anything with their woman unless she does all of the planning. If he doesn't want to plan anything for the weekend, that doesn't mean he doesn't love you. Some men just don't know how to plan out a weekend. Some men know how to plan an entire weekend, whether it is going to the park, to a high school game on a Friday night, or to a college game on a Saturday or an NFL game on Sunday, or just watching the game on television. He may plan to take the kids to a movie or to some other event. Some men don't do any of these things. This is why it's very important for you to do a background check on the man. There are many things that you can check out before getting into a relationship with a man. Does he gamble? Is he a loser when it comes to gambling? Will he lose all of his money? Why does he gamble? All of this can play a major part in a relationship with you even if you are a gambler too. You both may have a problem and need counseling.

One woman said to me that if she was looking for a man, he would have to first and foremost believe in God. He would have to be an honest, dependable person whom she could trust. He would have to be a positive person. He would have to be more of a people-centered person and not a materialist person, and he would have to be funny. She said most importantly, he would have to be her "highlighter," bringing out the very best in her. All of this is what she wanted from a man. How is she going to find this in a man? The only way she is going to know this about a man is to do a background check on him. Now, this is what she wants from man. What is she giving in return? Will she be giving all of her body to him? If she gives him her mind, she won't have anything to control the body.

Women, you need to see if the man you are looking for has some of the things you are looking for out of life. How do you know that he is the right man for you? There are a lot of ways to find out whether or not he is the right one for you. The right way to find out is by doing a background check on him. Men will sometimes try to get a woman to do things that they know are wrong for them to do just to see if they will do them. If you do those things, then he will know how to do things to you. Women let their hearts think for them and not their minds. That's when they make their mistakes by letting their hearts do their thinking for them. Always let your mind do the thinking for you. If you don't, you are going to think the wrong way in your relationship. Remember, mind first and heart second in everything you are intending to do in a relationship. Your heart can easily get the mind into the wrong situation. With a man, if you are planning on being with him for the rest of your life and you are a gold digger just out for what you can get out of him, then you aren't going by what your heart tells you. It's all based on materialistic things. You are out for what you can get in a relationship. It's all about what your eyes see before you, which are materialistic things.

If you are depending on a man, you will always go through life depending on someone else to help you through life. It is not good for you to be dependent on other people. Most of the time, this happens with women who are from a low-income family. They tend to think that men are supposed to take care of them, and that is the wrong way to be in life. Their moms may have let a man take care of all of their needs in the home, and they grow up thinking that's the way life is supposed to be. If you are self-supporting, then it's not a problem with you getting a man in your life. If you are looking for a man to take care all of your needs, you may have to look longer. There are only a few men out there these days who would be willing to take care of all of your needs, but not many.

Don't expect too much from your man. If you are giving, then you can expect him to give too. It's not all about you. It's about both of you giving to each other. This is why there are so many prenuptial agreements before marriage.

Some men don't care if you marry them for their money. What he doesn't want is you telling him some four to five years later that you want a divorce and trying and get half of what he owns. This is what he doesn't want. It's scary for him to marry without a prenuptial agreement. If you love him for him, then it should not be a problem. Men know that women marry them for what they have, and that's what men work so hard for to take care of the woman.

Men with money can pick from the tree because they have what most women want. Most women want a supportive man. A man knows this is true, so most of the time he can have his choice of who he wants. It's important for you to stay on your level and pick from the right tree. It's not too hard to do if you are doing a background check on the man that you are thinking about spending the rest of your life with.

Women, don't feel good about a man asking you out to dinner, because if you go when he first asks you, it may not be good for you. If you live on the same street as he does, still do a background check on him. When you are alone, most men will stay away from you, especially if you are more financially secure than he is. These may be the men who want to be in control of their women. If they can't be controlling, then they most likely won't try to make contact with a woman. Some men are living in the old days and can't get it out of their minds, and they think women are to be controlled. This is the way they see it in their minds. When you meet a man like this, he has been around for a while. He doesn't know any better.

Women, don't take men for granted. Some women are always asking what a man can do for them and not what they can do for him. Don't think of what he can do for you all of the time. Think of what you can do for him too. A relationship is about two people who care about each other and who are willing to work with each other together in the relationship. When you can do these things with each other, there is no limit to what you can do with each other. A relationship is about two people willing to help each other and share their love with each other. It's not about one in the relationship. This is why most relationships don't work out today. Someone in the relationship is more about self. This relationship will not work because thinking about only you will soon fade away.

In the past women were afraid of men, but today men are afraid of women in a relationship. This is how it is with men, and this is something that women should know about. Men in a relationship are afraid to let women know how much they care about a woman. A man is scared of losing her. He refuses to tell her how much he loves her and is willing to do for her. This is why it's so important to do a background check on the man so that you can be sure that this is the man you want for the rest of your life. A prenuptial agreement is okay if you are in love with this man. You aren't going to try to take him for everything he has. Let a man know up front that you are interested in his love and that's all you are asking of him. Some women shop too much. If you are one of these women, you should tell the man that you are. He may not want a woman who is always in the store spending money on clothes. He may want a woman who is into saving for the future. There are a lot of things that you should consider in a relationship before you get into a relationship with a man, because it's hard to get out when you are too far in.

Some men don't want to let go. One thing that I know for sure is that when women are finished with a relationship, they are finished. It's much different with a man when you are trying to get out of the relationship with him. You women need to know about men. A man will ease out of a relationship because he doesn't want the relationship anymore. You should not ever tell a man that you have someone else in your life and you are trying to get him out of your life. You are playing with your life. He just might go off at anytime. Don't ever make that mistake with him until you have him out of your life completely. You may try moving to another city. Be special to him until you can get him out of your life. This means you may need to get to a place where no one knows where you live but your mom. If she likes him and doesn't think he's the man you have been telling her about, he just may try to sweet talk her into telling him where you live. Keep away from your friends also until you hear that he has someone else in his life. Then you can go on with your life.

If you have any kids by him, sit them down and talk to them about the problem. If they already know the problem you have been having with him, they will be glad that you are trying to move on with your life. Men know how to get to kids by saying the things that they like to hear. They will say anything they think the children want to hear. If a man has been a father to them, he may not try this.

A man's heart is not as strong as a woman's heart, because women will have problems, but they will get past them sooner. I was talking with a woman about her divorce from her husband. She said that she had not been with a man for some twelve years and that her life was moving in another direction. She said it wasn't about a man. That shows that some women can go without a man. If you are a woman who feels as if you have to have a man in your life, then you just may get the same kind of man you just got away from. So you must put more time into searching for another man. Men aren't like women. They will go and get the first woman that looks like she may be available. In a man's mind, you weren't the woman for him. This is the way some men think. It's all about their pride. These are some of the things that you must think about when you are getting into a relationship with a man. If he has been married before, you need to check him out very well if you want the right man in your life. He could be someone who has an abusive background with women. I continue to say you must do the background check on him. It can be a problem for you if you don't do a background check.

Women, please be aware of good looks and gifts that are being offered to you. Sometimes those things can get you into something that you may have a problem getting away from. Don't accept too many things that you aren't able to give back the way it was given to you. If you have to go buy it new just to give it back the way he gave it to you, do so. If you break it off with him, you may upset him because he feels that all of the things he has given you should be repaid. This is when restraining orders come into play. You must work this relationship out with him to keep from having to do press charges against him in the long run.

Women in abusive relationships end up in a divorce. Sixty percent of divorce cases end up in a tragic relationship. Some 40 percent end up in bitter relationships. So, you need to do a background check. It doesn't work sometimes, but you know what this man is about by doing a background check on him. Most men want to be a husband, but they don't trust like they need to. The little things that their wives do and say to them are what makes them afraid to open up the way they want to. This is the same for a single man when he meets a woman, because he doesn't want to be in a relationship. Men don't want to be with someone who is not happy. Women need to be very straight with men when they meet one. If you don't, you may end up with the kind of relationship that ends up abusive or tragic.

Most men who are always telling you things about yourself may not be for you. If a man is always saying little things to you to humiliate you, like "Why do you have that short dress on?" or "Why are you sitting around with make-up on in the house?" or "Where have you been?" you may just have the hots for him. This is how it is for some women. He isn't comfortable with himself and he is afraid of losing you to someone else. What you need to do with this type of man is tell him how much you love him every day of the week if you want to have a good relationship with him.

I know that a woman doesn't want to have sex all of the time with her husband, but if it takes this to make your husband happy, then that's what you do. If you are in love with him and this makes your marriage work, then do it. Now, this is not the case for single women. If you are not married, you do not need to have sex with him (all of the time). If he loves you and wants you, he will do whatever it takes to keep you. You need to hold out (to some degree) when it comes to what it is he wants most. Now, if you aren't having sex with him until you get married, he may not go for that. However, there will be one that will come along and be willing to wait. He will do whatever it takes because he wants you. He will be all right with you holding back. If you hold off with him for six months or so, it will make a difference. If he is visiting you often and making you happy, he may try to have sex with you every time he sees you. You tell him that you love him but you aren't going to have sex with him until you are married. You don't have to have sex with a man when you meet him unless you are the one wanting to have sex with him.

You are making a mistake because men think differently than women. If a man takes a woman out and she has sex with him on the first or second date, then he sees her as a little promiscuous. He won't think much of you. He may think that the first man you meet you will have sex with. Now, not all men think this way. Some will just try to keep a watch on you to see if you are seeing someone else. This will give him a chance to move on with his life. Women who are out there looking for someone to have in their lives should take their time. Don't worry about all of your friends who have a husband. Some of your friends may wish they were like you. They may be in a bad relationship with their husband and want out. Just because a friend may act like she is happy with her marriage doesn't mean she really is.

Young ladies out there who are in high school and middle school should not let a young man get too close, such as having sex. He is going to tell his friends what happened between the two of you. The next thing you know, all of the other ladies don't like you, because one of them may have been with this young man as well. You may have been with one of their boyfriends. You may end up with one of these ladies wanting to fight you because you have been having sex with their boyfriend.

If you are a young girl, hold on to your body because your body should be precious to you. You shouldn't lose it (your virginity) to just anyone. It should be your husband when you are out of school. You must be a respectful person throughout your school years. You will carry respect with you all the way through life. It starts in middle school. It isn't a good thing for you to lose your body (virginity) to someone because of the different kinds of diseases. A long time ago, there weren't that many diseases (that we knew of) in America. When I was growing up, there were a few different types of sexually transmitted diseases. Today there are many different kinds of sexually transmitted diseases out there. So what I am telling you young women and men is that you need to start where you are supposed to start, and that is by not having sex or using a condom.

I once heard someone say to me that young kids today think that they are not having sex when they have oral sex. I have heard that kind of sex is not supposed to be for humans. Women, if you don't take care of your body, who will. Your parents can tell you some things about taking care of your body, but ultimately, when it comes down to it, it is your responsibility to take care of your body. If you don't take care of your body, no one else will. I am saying that women need to take control of their bodies and not let anyone else take control of their minds or bodies. Don't let a man control your body or mind. I am concerned about young women today because it seems to me that young men are taking over young women's bodies and minds. I knew a woman who was afraid to speak to men because of the problems she would have

47

with her husband for speaking to another man. This is not the kind of life you want to have. By doing a background check on him, you will save yourself a lot of heartache in the future.

Some men are insecure with themselves, and it's hard for some men to get a woman and keep her. When he does get one, he doesn't want to let her go. This is why you should be careful when you are out there looking for a man. Women, there are plenty of men out there in this country. You have to look in the right places for them. If you find your man inside of a bar, then you may have a man who's going to be in the bar all of the time. This is why you should do all of the things you need to do to check him out before getting too seriously involved.

I have heard men say things about women that I knew. They think that all women will do the same thing when they are out in the night life. They think when women are out in the bars and in the clubs at night they all act the same way. They don't think about some of the respectful women who are only out to have a good time. For some men it's hard to get over a woman if she has been disrespectful to them. They feel that all women are the same. This is another reason why women have to be careful where they find their man. I'm not saying that if you find one in the church, you don't have to be as careful, because you do. The kind of man that you may be looking for in life may not be the man for you. He may just be the worst man that you have ever dated. His background check will tell you all of the things that you need to know about him. Position yourself in a place to better your chances of finding a man that you want for life.

If you are a woman who believes in the Almighty, God, you will have goodness in your life. There are more good men today than there are bad ones. Some women attract the men who aren't special to women, meaning they are all about themselves in a relationship. Women, when you get a man like this, there's nothing that you can do about it, but don't get involved. Do what is best for you.

When you have a man who goes into a rage when you aren't where he thinks are supposed to be, then don't do the things that are going to set him off. The best thing for you to do is to do the best thing that you can do toward him until you can get it together for yourself and leave him. I am telling you these things because you need to know them.

Once there was a woman who left her friend and went to another city to live, and the man found out where she was through her mom telling someone she worked with, not knowing that this woman even knew anything about this man. The woman went back and told the man where she was at that time. Now, the man didn't try to see this woman again, because he didn't want her to know that he knew where she was. He wanted to see her, but not the way most men want to see a woman. He wanted to see her to tell her that he was sorry about their misunderstanding and that it would not ever happen again. They eventually talked and worked through their problems. If he had told someone where she was at that time, it may have spooked her and she could have run again. These two people are doing just fine with each other today and are married with a son. They have been together for some twenty years!

Sometimes it takes some women longer to find the man of their dreams than it does other women. That's just the way it is for some women. In earlier years, you didn't find low-income families getting divorced. Time has changed things today with women and men. Women have their own jobs and their own cars. During earlier years, most women didn't work. Men did most all of the work with your big companies. Men had more control over women then. In today's world there is a new order. Some men can't live with this new order. This kind of man is mad at the world about his own life and does not want to live by the new order. In earlier years women couldn't go to someone for much, because it had to go through her husband. If it was against her husband's wishes, she couldn't get anything done.

Some fifty years later, it is different with women. Now 75 percent of women tell their husbands what to do in their households. These families are those most likely to do well in their relationships. Women have all of the advantages today in a relationship with a man because you don't need him for anything. Women need someone to tell them that they are loved and to be comforted. Why should you accept anything other than what you deserve from a man when you don't have to? Women will say they don't know how to date someone else because they have been together with one other person for so long. Well, if you want to get out of a relationship, you will do whatever it takes to leave that relationship. You can get out of the relationship the right way. Don't be afraid to get out of a relationship.

Some women are always giving their men an ultimatum in their relationship. Some men don't *do* ultimatums. For example, you might tell your man that if he doesn't stop staying out late at night you are going to leave him or get someone else to stay at home with you. Now, this is the wrong thing to tell your man. An ultimatum is not the thing to say to him when he is not being 100 percent with you. This is why this book is for women only. It is not for men. Men will not understand this book because it's not for them to understand; it is only for you to understand. This book was written so that you will understand men and how to get up with them.

There was a woman who gave her man an ultimatum about the house they were living in and having her name on the house. She went missing. Some weeks later she was found in a lake. This is why you don't say things to your man when you know he may be abusive to you.

Some men think that if they can't have you, then no one else will. It's scary today with some men because they are demanding and women are involved in more abusive relationships than ever before. It's a sign when you meet a man that's abusive to women and when you find a man that's not married. If he is in his forties and has not been married, you really need to check him out. I am not saying that something is wrong with him. I'm saying that you need to check him out well. You may find out why he's not been married.

Women, men aren't trying to find a wife, because why should they get married when they can find a woman most anywhere if they look okay and have a good job? Then they get what they need from a woman to satisfy their needs. So you need to hold on to your body when you meet a man. If you let him have his way with your body, he will most likely be coming back to see if you are real about your body. If you aren't doing these things with the man in your life you are dating, you need to stop having sex with him until you get what you want out of the relationship. This will keep happening as long as a man can get what he wants from you without marrying you. Men aren't like women. Almost all men want to have a night with their woman. It's different with women because this is not the way for women. How do you stop it? You determine when you are going to have sex with your man. This is the most important way. There are some other ways, but this is the main way.

It's hard for a woman not to do this with a man that she really cares about. If you can continue to not have sex with him, he will soon ask you to marry him if he cares enough about you. Wait until he gives you a ring, letting you know that he really wants you for the rest of his life and that he really wants you for you and not for what he can get from you. The background check will make it work out for you.

Women shouldn't always look in the front for what they can get sometimes around the corner. What's best for you may be straight ahead, but it doesn't work out to be the best sometimes. Most of the time, it doesn't work for you because you don't know what's behind it. This is why it's very important for you to do a background check on the person that you are interested in. If you are a person willing to do any and everything for him that he asks of you, then that might not be too good for you in the relationship. He will begin to think that you will do whatever he tells you to do just because you are in love with him with all of your heart and mind. It is not good for him to think that way about you. This is when he will begin to think that he can control you. Now, when you are not doing these things for him, he will begin to think that he is going to lose you. He doesn't want that.

It all started from the first time that you met him, when you were doing everything that he would ask of you. This isn't the way to go with a man. Start the relationship the way you want to keep it with him. Most relationships don't work out for more than two or three years. Today the world is moving too fast for people. People are trying to keep up with time and the changes brought on by time. You can't keep up with all of the changes that are going on in the world today. You must not try to keep up with your friends or with their style of living. Let it go and live your style of your life and you will see the difference in your everyday living.

When I was a young man growing up, I would hear people say they were trying to keep up with the Joneses.

Keeping up with the Joneses or keeping up with someone who is financially able to have expensive things can drive you in a hole. Seventy-five percent of African Americans try to live this way. Most people are living from one check to the next. When women try to live this way, it puts too much pressure on your man. You are supposed to have fun. You are not supposed to be drained with high expenses. This isn't the way to live with your man. Living according to your means is important. At the end of the year, you will see a difference in your day-to-day living. You should save thousands of dollars each year. This will create a successful marriage.

I watched an Oprah show that was about men and women and intimate sex. What women need to know is that men don't have the same feelings that women have about sex. One of the men on the show said that men aren't likely to be able to touch and play like women can and not have sex. Women can get touchy and play and not have sex. Men get reared up and ready to have sex, and women don't. The show also discussed how some men sleep with other women and do not care for the other women they have sex with. This is not the case with women. When a woman has sex with another man, she usually has to have feelings for him to have sex with him. Some men can be getting all that the woman can give at home, and at the same time, they will go outside of the home and have sex with another woman.

Some men can't stand or fight temptation when it comes down to being with another woman. This is not all men, just some men. Men don't think like women. When it comes to losing what they have at home, men will take that chance. When it comes to having sex with another woman, he doesn't want to lose what he has at home, but he thinks that he can take a chance and be with another woman. He thinks that his woman at home won't find out about him having sex with another woman. Sometimes the man's uncontrollable sex mind will be the number-one thing that will send him out on the street looking for another woman. If a woman can keep herself "on" all of the time for her man, then there's a chance that he won't go out in the street to look for another woman. One of the things he will think is that he is not pleasing her.

Women, trying to find a perfect man is hard to do in this day and time. You will find a man who's respectful to you and who will try to do all the things that a man is supposed to do for his woman. Women, when you find a man that you think is the man for you and you find out that he isn't being true to you, you need to kick him out of your life. If not, he will continue to do these things to you. You will continue to forgive him. This will most likely end up being a bad relationship. I read in the *New York Times* that a woman said that she didn't see why it was so hard for teachers and nurses in San Francisco to get a man. She said that she was going to build some condominiums in a middle-class neighborhood. She said that some women get past their thirties and seem to have a problem getting married. They get set in their own ways. It's hard for them to change to meet someone else's needs. This is why you will see that there are a lot of women who aren't married after their thirtieth birthday.

They usually get used to being alone and doing whatever they want whenever they want. I am not saying that they don't want to get themselves a husband, but they aren't going to change their lifestyle for a man. This is why some women go around saying that there are no good men out there. There are no men out there who are willing to live by their rules.

A relationship is supposed to be based on two people, not just one person. If you both agree that this is the way a relationship is supposed to go, then it will work for you. Women should do a good background check on men they are going to have in her life. Some women aren't looking for but one thing and that is a man who is going to take care of her. This is not the way it is supposed to be in life. It's supposed to be two people making it together. Sometimes it's best for a woman to get married right after she graduates from college, because if she goes too long, she will get comfortable living alone. Sometimes it takes a while for them to get a husband, not because there isn't anyone out there. It's because there is no one out there willing to live their life the way someone else wants them to. Women are looking for the wrong things from a man. Looks and integrity are very rare. Hopefully you will find integrity, good looks, smarts, and wealth. It doesn't have to be him owning his own business; just a man with integrity and smarts is really all that should be required.

Some men these days are different than they were ten years ago. Times change every ten years or so. If you look back over the last ten years, you will see times are different. The world is moving too fast for some people, and they get caught up in this fast world. They can't turn themselves lose because they are hooked on it. It's just like a person on drugs who is having a hard time getting away from them.

I studied this song that a bishop wrote, which is about the world moving too fast. If you take time out and listen to this song, you will get some sense out of what he is saying in this song. I also like to listen to a song that he wrote that is about God "raining down a blessing." In New Orleans, most of the people received a blessing from the hurricane. The people in Mississippi received a blessing too. A blessing comes in many different ways for people. If a woman waits on a man to come into her life, he will come into your life.

There are many ways that you can meet the right man to spend the rest of your life with. There was this man and woman who worked for the same company as a man she was interested in. They were not supposed to date each other. The two of them had feelings for each other. This went on for about four years. Finally the woman said that she'd had enough and went to her supervisor and told her that she had feelings for someone at work. She told her that she was going to marry him and couldn't work for the company anymore. After all of those years, she knew that she had the man she wanted to be with for the rest of her life. She took advantage of it by letting her job go.

When a man gets into a relationship with a woman, he sometimes doesn't want to be as serious as the woman in the relationship. Men grow into the relationship and women are serious the minute they meet a man. It's hard for a woman to tell how much a man loves her. It will take some time before she can tell about the relationship with him. This is why you should take it easy with your heart. Don't give him sex. See if he will be willing to accept that from you. Every time you call him, get him to say that he loves you with all of his heart. If he doesn't say these things to you, maybe he is seeing someone else. Don't try to make him say it to you. You'll know when he is alone or if he's with the guys. He will always say it differently if he is with the guys. Most young men won't tell you how much they love you on the phone if their friends are around. When you ask a man if he loves you, he will say yeah .

This is for single women, not for married women. When he comes around, get dressed and tell him that you are going out with friends. If he asks you where you are going, tell him you are going to a bar with some friends he doesn't know. I am not saying go out and look for someone. Just put something in his mind to see how he will take it. There are a lot of ways to see where a man's heart is. Sometimes love is like a job. You have to work at a relationship. You look at the caller ID and see that it's him. Don't answer. See how many times he'll call you back. If he doesn't call you back, it may be a sign that you need to let him go unless there was some reason that he didn't call you back. It's not always that you have to see him with someone else. There are other ways for you to figure out whether or not he is being true to you. It doesn't have to be a huge misunderstanding when you find out he isn't the man for you. Send him an email letting him know. Don't let him know that you are going out to get yourself another man.

I know this man who had thirteen women he was seeing. He would tell all of them that he loved them. So, for some men, telling you that they love you is easy. This isn't the question to ask him. You tell him that if you find out he is seeing someone else, there will no longer be a relationship between the two of you. You can find out about your man. If he is seeing someone else, he will slip up by being with her. He will come home with perfume on his clothing. When you get close to him, check out his clothes to see if he has been with someone else. You are in the relationship to make it last, not to be playing around.

Women, you are supposed to be the head of the relationship. Men don't think of all the exciting places you will think of to have a romantic evening. Women will sit around with their coworkers trying to decide where they should take their friend on his birthday. A man will just say that he's taking you out tonight for your birthday. He may take you to a local restaurant where you usually go most of the time. All men aren't like that, so don't think this way about all men. Women are looking for a man to fulfill their needs, to love and romance them, or to help them with their finances.

Sometimes we can understand each other when we live as one if we let the other into our hearts and minds. This is how it's supposed to be with the love of your life after you have did your background check and it checks out the way you want it to check out for you. When going out with someone new, you should always go to a restaurant in an area where most of the people know you.

Some men want to control their women. This is what you need to watch out for in a man, because he just may be the kind of man who is controlling. If there are evident signs of him trying to control you, you should let him know that he is controlling and you don't want a controlling man in your life. This is when most women get weak with men because they begin to feel bad about what they have said to him. Men have a way of manipulating women when they find themselves in trouble with women. What a man does is bring up the things that he knows are going to get next to you to get him out of the situation. He will get you upset, and you will forget what you had said to him. Don't let this happen to you. Don't let him turn the situation around on you.

When a man knows that his woman loves him, she will not leave him or let him leave her. Most men know how to turn the conversation on his woman. When a woman tells a man that he hasn't been true, she shouldn't let him turn the guilt on her. Men aren't going to answer you when you ask them if they have been cheating. The only way that a man will say that he has been cheating on you is if you say that you are going to the person to ask her or if you say that you are leaving him. Some of them still won't say they have been cheating.

Some men won't tell you that he loves you every day, so don't think that your man doesn't love you because he doesn't tell you every day. When he leaves for work, if he tells you that he loves you, then most likely he isn't going to cheat on you. The ones who are always saying these things to you are the ones that you need to watch. It's good for him to tell you that he loves you when he leaves for work. Some men are into kissing all of the time. Some men don't want their women pulling on them and kissing on them. Men in their late forties and older see it differently than younger men. Older men are more conscious of kissing because of oral sex. In the past, older black men didn't get into oral sex. However, the young black men have gotten into it just like all of the other races of people. Some men don't like oral sex. Back in the fifties, if you were a man that had oral sex with a woman, people wouldn't want to be around you. If you set your glass down, they would slide the glass away from them. I know about black men because I'm one of them. I am an older black man who was brought up during these days.

There are some women in their early fifties and sixties who haven't had oral sex. This kind of sexual relationship with a man is something new to them. Some men are like the moon; they change some four times a month or more. So, women, you can't base your relationship with this man on other men you may know, because they may be two different kinds of men.

There was this woman who had everything going for herself in life. She loved her husband and wanted all of him. She just couldn't believe that he was loving someone else while being married to her. She left him alone and bought herself the most expensive penthouse that she could get in the city. Her love for him turned into hate and it drove her over the edge to killing him. She plotted to kill him and did. You can't let love get you this way. A woman can give too much to the one she loves and not think about what she needs from him.

You are the woman and are supposed to tell him the things you want to do in the relationship. Some men win you over and forget how they won you over. They forget to make you happy at all times. Some men love their wives more after marriage because you are his everything to him. When you get married, don't let the relationship go downhill. Keep it going up. There is no limit to how far it can grow if you keep the fire burning in the relationship. When the fire goes out, it's hard to get it going again. You may get it going, but it won't be the same. There may be something in the relationship that is missing with you both. So it's mandatory that you both keep the relationship on fire with each other. When you as the woman see this relationship slowing down, you should add a little spark to the relationship if you want to keep it going for the both of you.

Love is just like a car. If you don't keep up the maintenance on the car, it will soon start to deteriorate, and it will take a lot of work to get it back in good working condition. Love is like a job. When you go to work every day, you must do the job like the company wants you to do it. It will show whether you are qualified to do the job and what is expected of you. If you can't do the job, the company won't operate properly, so you will cause the company to operate below expectations and will eventually be fired. Everything is based on a format.

Love never gets old. You may make it old if you stop working at it. If you stop working on a job every day, you will soon not have a job anymore. It is shameful to stop working on love if you are involved in a relationship. It sometimes will not work for you, but continue to work on your relationship in order to make it work for you.

Things will not stay the same if you don't continue working on it. If you don't continue to work in your yard, it will soon look like no one lives there. If you don't continue to keep your house in good condition, it will soon start to look run down. If you don't take care of your health, it will soon deteriorate. So it is important to keep working on your relationship with your partner. If you are dating, it is the same for you too. I was watching *The View* one morning and they were talking about how a woman had glued a man's rectum together and some of his other body parts as well. She decided that she didn't want to work anymore at the relationship. These are some of the things that will happen in a relationship if you don't work on it. Women, you can't change your man. If he is set in his ways, you can work on helping him with that. Some men think that women are supposed to tell them everything, and they aren't supposed to tell them anything but what they want to tell them. If you have a man like this, you need to get away from him as soon as you can because you are living a miserable life. This isn't the way marriage is supposed to be. Some women will get married and some years later will get a divorce. This is not good for you because people will begin to say it must be you in the relationship. You don't want people to begin to talk about you like that.

A high-profile woman shouldn't care what people think about her in a relationship with a man, but it's different with a woman who doesn't have a high profile. I know some women who are in a new relationship with a man every six months. I know a woman who has her doctorate degree and she can't keep a relationship with a man. She has had high-profile men and some who are not high profile. Since I have known her, all of the men she dates seem like good men from what I hear. I think she was treated wrong when she was a little girl growing up with her dad at home. When a young girl has been used to having her way all of her childhood days with her parents, then it will be hard for her to change her lifestyle with someone else. She will be looking for that man to treat her the way her dad has always treated her. It may be that he's not the same as the father figure that she is accustomed to.

I know another woman who is highly educated. She has a master's degree in math. She is a teacher and she has a problem with men. She is a woman who's a daddy's girl. This makes it hard for women when they grow up. They think that their men are supposed to treat them the same way their dad treated them while they were living at home. Women, don't always wait for the man to ask to take you out. You can ask him to go out to a restaurant sometimes. Some men will appreciate that from you. This works too if you are married. There is nothing wrong with doing these things for the man that you care for. Some of you women want a man to do everything for you just because you have a body to give him when you want him to have it. Then some of you think that's the way it's supposed to go. It's time for some of you women to catch up in the world today. I heard this recording my bishop sang one day and I thought about what he was saying in the song. The song was about how the world is moving much too fast. Some of you women are moving much too fast. In your life today, you don't see what you are getting into with a relationship. I have heard some women with all kinds of degrees meet men and sleep with him on the same night. This is a woman who is lonely and needs attention. Some women are trying to see how many men they can play. Now, this is not the case with this woman. She is missing that one little thing in her life that she left back at home with her parents, and she won't ever find it until she gets some counseling in her life about her relationships with men. The way she is living her life, she can meet the wrong man in her life because of what she has been missing in her life. When she can't get her way with men, it's her way or no way. It's not going to work all of the time with some men and that's what the problem with women is. She is ready to go, and he's not ready for her to go. This is how a misunderstanding between two people comes about. They aren't thinking about the way it's supposed to end, because there is no understanding in the beginning with the both of you in the relationship. Some women sleep with men the first time they meet them, and these women are what you would call your sophisticated hood rats.

Sophisticated hood rats aren't supposed to do the same thing that the hood rats do in life. I find there to be more sophisticated hood rats that sleep with men the first time than your ordinary hood rats. The hood rats will be quick to say to a man "What do you think I am, a whore?" Then, they will shut the door in your face. It's somewhat different with a sophisticated hood rat. Most women are the same way, only in different ways. Some women like to do things like go for a walk in the park or go to a movie on the weekend. I am not telling you how to keep your man. I am telling you what to do when you meet a man. Wherever you meet him, it doesn't make any difference because you have some of the same types of men everywhere you go. You need to know him when you see him.

These men are looking for weak women with a large bank account. This is why you should always do a background check on the man you are getting involved with. If you find a man in the world that does not meet your standards, don't waste your time. You may want to reevaluate your set of standards. Do you take it or leave it? If you leave it, then you may have missed the man of life. Don't always look for the highest standards in a man. Look for integrity in a man. Look for a man who has morals in life. Some men don't have these things in life and have no intention of having any.

Some men think bad about women. What about the women who are in show business? There is nothing said about them and their life choices, such as getting married four or five times. What's the difference between getting married all of the time and dating four or five men at the same time? Over a period of time, if she does these things, she will be considered a whore.

Live by the rule of your country. Have integrity for yourself because no one else will. Have respect for your body, heart, and soul. The mind is the delivery system for the body. When you meet a man, you must put your mind into it. Use nothing else but your mind. If you let the heart in before the mind, you are in for failure. Your heart is only there for the body to keep it flowing for the body. Keep your eyes and ears open so that you can listen closer to everything that is said.

Oprah is one of the most famous women in the world who is not married. She can marry any man that she wants. She has chosen not to marry anyone. Why is the most highly respected woman in the world single? Oprah is one of the richest women in the world and maybe one of the most unhappy women in the world. Watching her shows each and every day, you would think that she is the happiest woman in the world. One thing for sure is that for those watching her show, she makes it look like she's the happiest person in the entire world.

Things can happen in your life and knock you down. It doesn't mean you should stay down. It means you should get up and try it again. Some critics will tell you that you can't get back, and if you listen to what they tell you, then you have no mind of your own because you have given up on your own mind, and for the rest of your life you will be listening to someone else tell you what to do with your mind, so don't let some man take away of your mind, because all you have is your mind. Without it you have nothing to carry you on in life but your body, and what is it without your mind? Nothing.

Once I said to myself that I wasn't going to listen to what someone said to me. I did just what I said I was going to do. If you say that you aren't going to do something again that you have done before, you need to keep your word. If you are not on the right path in life, it will happen again. I have heard women say that they are not going to get another man like that again, and they end up with one who's worse. It doesn't happen that way with all women. Some women say "I hope and trust in my God that I don't get into another relationship like I had before." The difference is in the way it was said about the relationships.

Most of these things just happen with them for no reason at all. I am not saying anything to people who are not into the same religion. I am talking about the way some think about the situation. When you are skeptical about someone, you need to always do a background check. This is all about you being happy with the man in your life. This is your mind, not your heart. When you are relying on your mind, it will guide you the right way in life with a little help along the way. Sometimes it's best to wait until you have dated some men.

I listen to women and their needs in life. The problem that they have is low self-esteem. When your self-esteem is down, you have no control over your mind and body. Anyone can get control of your body. It can be your sister or your brother. I am telling you this can happen to you because it has been done with this one sister I know. She controls her other sister's relationships. If she doesn't like the man her sister is dating, she will find a way to break them up.

When someone thinks that he has you under his control, he will take control of your life. I heard this woman tell a judge once that her husband would come home late and tell her to get up from out of the bed and go and sleep on the sofa. This man continued to do these kinds of things to her and she stayed with him. She had low self-esteem. He continued to tell her that she was helpless. She began to think that was the way she was. He was taking control of her mind. This is what some men do to their women. I have known some men who wouldn't let their women go out of the house. Some women can't do anything without their man's consent. They can't go out with their friends at any time. Some men will turn their woman against their own family for no reason.

When a woman has a man like this, she needs to let him know that he can't turn her against her family or her friends that she had before she met him. These are the kinds of things that happen with women, and they don't know that it's wrong. I feel sorry for her because she doesn't know that her mind has been taken by the unknown man. Women, you got to take control of your relationship with a man by letting him know that you have your own mind to tell you when to go and when to stay, and all you need from him is for him to treat you like you are his woman and nothing else. If not, you need to be moving on with your life because you aren't going to let him take control of your mind and heart, because if you do, then what will you have? A background check is what you need to do. It doesn't make any difference how he comes on to you. Your job is to do a background check on this man. When you decide not to do a background check on the man, you will slip up with this man because he could be a rapist or a serial killer.

There are a lot of good men out there. If you are looking in the right places for a man, you may find him anywhere. It could be at a gas station or maybe at a store. You never know where you may meet him. I met my second wife at a nightclub one Sunday evening. I was riding around that evening with no shirt on and saw this young lady standing on the outside of the club. I was talking with someone for a while, and all of a sudden this woman came out of the club and she took my breath away. I asked the person I was talking to if she knew who the young woman was, and she didn't know her. Well, that's where we met, and we've been together ever since that day. It has been twenty-two years. I am not saying that I have been the best man that I could have been, but we have managed to make it work for the both of us.

Sometimes when you are out in the world looking for someone special or just someone to have fun with, it doesn't have to be someone that you are dating. There is nothing wrong with going out to a movie sometimes. This is what women need to do if they aren't married. You can get a better feel for men if you go out with a man that's a friend to you, because he can give you good advice about other men. If he is your true friend, he will do this because he doesn't want you to choose the wrong man. You just may hold him responsible. It's always good for a woman to have a man friend in her life because he will tell you the truth about other men. A woman friend may be a little different about telling you the truth about the man in your life or about a man that you are interested in, because most women don't want to hurt their friend. If she isn't your friend, then she will tell you just to hurt your feelings about the man you are interested in. So, it's always good to have a true man friend that you can talk to. This is not to say that women will not tell each other the truth; I am just saying have a man friend in the background so that you can go to him about situations involving other men. He will always try to help the best way he can. If he can't help at the present time, he will think on it and get back to you about the situation! If you want to know about a man, you can get better advice by going to a man. Make sure he is a truthful man and that he doesn't want you for himself. You need to watch out for these men. If he wants you for himself, then he just might not tell you the truth about someone you are interested in.

If you are in school or on a job, try to keep a man friend that you can talk to. If you are a single woman living alone and don't have a man in your life, keep a close man friend nearby.

The first thing you need to know is not to date a married man. It doesn't make any sense to date married men with all of the men that are not married. You are going to waste your precious time by dating a married man. It doesn't bring about anything for you. On the holidays you are alone because he will be with his wife and family. You will be alone or imposing on others during the holiday season, thinking and wishing that the holiday would hurry up and pass. It will seem like the holidays are getting longer because you can't wait until you can see him again. This isn't the life for you. If you are a young or middle-aged woman, being with a married man isn't the way to go about your life.

If you continue to believe in yourself and put all of your trust in God, then you will find the love of your life. If you aren't patient enough to wait on someone, you may make the wrong choices in your life. You will want to blame it on the other person. It's you that you should hold responsible for your bad choices. You couldn't wait and just wanted a man. You couldn't wait for your man to come to you, so you reached and got some one else's man. These are some of the things that we don't want to deal with, but that's life. So what I am trying to do is to get women to learn about men. Sometimes you won't find a man on the same level that you are on. When you are looking for a man, you are looking for love and a companion in life. You are not looking for someone to totally take care of you. Today is a different world; it's the new millennium. You must look for love and happiness from a man. There was a time when women would go out looking for a man who would take care of them. It's not that way anymore in the new millennium. It's about the both of you taking care of each other and taking care of your finances together.

It's hard for us sometimes. Life is not supposed to be easy. It's what we make it out to be. Don't be deceived by a man full of tricks and teasing. It's one thing to live in poverty, but living in poverty for love and not having enough love to go on is your imagination. When your mind gets to you, then you begin to make the wrong decisions because you no longer are listening to your mind. You begin to let your mind take over you. It's not uncommon for this to happen to people. So, if this is happening to you, then you need to take back control of your life.

We have six senses that control our minds. When they begin to weaken, we have to fight to gain control of our minds. It's just like an automobile trying to perform with seven sparkplugs, but it needs eight sparkplugs to operate. Keep your mind in check when you are out trying to get the man of your dreams. When you find the right man in your life, don't ask him if he is cheating on you. If you think he is cheating, then go out and hire a private investigator to see if he is really cheating. There are many things you can do that can help you in your relationship. It's the same when you meet someone that you are planning to date. Have a background check done for you. In the new millennium. Women have all the rights and can do most anything that they want to do in life. We have women commentators in the sports, working everywhere, doing everything. Women have all the chances to find a good man if they go out and do a background check on the man they are looking to date.

Just in case you don't already know this, you aren't going to find the perfect man. There is no such thing as a perfect man if that's what you are looking for. Don't always say there aren't any good men out there or that all of the good men are married, because that's not true. You have some men saying the same about women. If you have a woman for your friend and she is married and her marriage isn't going too well, she will be a bad influence on you. Her impression of men will be bad and you will be skeptical about the man you meet. I am not saying don't have a married woman as a friend, but just don't go to her about your relationship with a man. If you have a woman friend who is married and her marriage is going just fine, then she will tell you there's no relationship like being married. You both have something special in life together, and that marriage is the best kind of life there is. Don't let anyone tell you that a single life is the best because you can go when you get ready. The key to a good relationship is when both of you are being true to one another. If you want to go out, you can, and it's not a problem for either of you.

When you find a good man, you won't have any problems keeping him if you are a good woman to him, because most men know it when they have a good woman. He isn't going to take any chances of losing you. Rich women live a different lifestyle than women who are not rich. They don't always get what they want, but something is better than nothing to them. Some women change men like some people change cars, every four years.

Women are the same when it comes to having someone to love and wanting someone to cherish them. They want someone who really cares about them and not just someone they had a mini-affair with in bed. Women want someone to come home to. Women want to be loved, and they don't want to wait on someone to get there to love them.

When you find a good man, you should treat him like you care about him. Don't wait for him to come on to you when you are in a passionate mood for love. Come on to him. Men love it when a woman comes on to him. If you are his wife—and you women need to know this about your man—when he comes home from work, meet him at the door with a kiss and whisper in his ear. Say things like "I am feeling a little sexy today and what are you going to do about it?" with a smile.

If you live alone, start taking his clothes off as soon as he closes the door to the house and lead him to the sofa or just pull him down on the floor. It doesn't make any difference when it is in your house. These are some of the things that you should do to keep up in a relationship with your husband or, if you are not married, your man. You can send a man out in the world looking for what he can't get at home with you. It's usually sex he's looking for out in the street, but he still loves you. Most women will say "If he loves me, why did he cheat on me?" He cheated because you weren't being affectionate to him by taking care of his needs. It's all about sex. If you continue to do these things, it will continue to happen with him. This isn't something that he wants, because he will see what it could lead up to: his marriage ending in divorce or separation. When you meet a man, you need to know about how he treats a woman, and if you decide to date him, you need to know him before you do some of these things with him. There are too many men out there that are rapists and murderers. This is why it's very important to do a background check.

On special days like birthdays, don't ask what he wants to do on his birthday. You are the person who's planning the event, so why should you ask him what he wants to do for his birthday? When you are planning events like that, it shows him the love that you have for him. He will be proud of you and know that you are thinking of him and caring for him, which will make him feel good. Just plan the event without asking him and tell him that you have something special for him. If you are married with kids, have a friend to keep the kids for the night when you have planned a special evening for him. If it's a school day, have the kids take their clothes with them for the next morning.

For you single women, it's the same way for you too. Do special things for him if you love him. Don't worry about what he didn't do for you on your birthday. Maybe he couldn't afford to do things for you that are as nice as what you did for him on his birthday. What's important is that he did something for you. That's what matters in the relationship. If he can afford to do these things, then that's different because there may be something wrong with the relationship. You may not be doing the things that you are supposed to be doing in the relationship. Remember what you did in the beginning when you first fell in love with each other.

If you are a woman who's dating, then the same thing goes for you to keep the relationship hot. If he doesn't want to keep it hot, then you must ask him if there's something wrong with you. If the answer is no, then it's time to do an investigation on him just to see if he is keeping it real in the relationship. Try to keep your appearance the same as you did when you met him. Always look good to him. It doesn't take that much effort, because he will see you when you are leaving for work in the mornings. In the evening when you get home from work, that's the time when you can take it all off and keep a little something on. This gives him the desire to hold you in his arms in the evening. This will get him in the mood when he is looking at you with your sexy clothes on. You may want to wear a short, loose dress with a low-cut top with your breasts showing just a little. Show just enough for him to see them peeping through. When you lean down to pick up something or to get something out of the cabinet, don't stoop. Bend over to get whatever you are getting or raise yourself up. These are some of the things that will keep your man's mind on you. When you do this to him, he will then move toward you because you have reminded him of something that he enjoys, which is having sex with you.

The love he has for you will grow. I am not saying that sex is what it is all about in the relationship, but it is 90 percent of the relationship. Now, this doesn't pertain to those who are married for convenience. I am talking about people who are married and who want to be happy in the relationship. If it's about convenience, then you don't really know about having a true relationship with someone. You only know about what makes you happy. That is fine, but sometimes life can get dark and you can't see how a relationship is benefiting you anymore.

Without love, health, happiness, friends, and having God in your life, you won't have anything or anyone.

These are some of the things that I wanted women to know about men!

The main thing in life is to know what you want from your relationship with a man!

Know who and what you want; it doesn't make any difference what your race is!

Know that you want a man to be special to you!

Know that you will be special to him!

Know that you will listen to what he has to say to you. If you don't think what he is saying is right, just listen to what he has to say anyway. It doesn't mean that you are going to agree with him; just listen!

Life is about you knowing yourself, and when you know yourself, there is nothing that you won't listen to, because you know yourself!

Being knowledgeable is the best thing in life!

It once was said that there was a rich woman who would walk her dog through her neighborhood every morning. One particular morning, she decided to take a shortcut through a black neighborhood. As she walked down the street, a sooner (dog) ran from behind the bushes and jumped on the top of her dog. She was yelling for help. A little black boy was standing on the corner with his finger in his mouth, watching the white woman. She said to the little boy, who was about seven years old, that he needed to stop watching and that he needed to be in school. He told her he knew how to get the dogs apart. Well, after no one came, the woman told the little boy to get them apart before the dog hurt her little Jennifer. The little boy took his other hand and wrapped it around the dog's his tail and rammed his finger, the same one he'd had in his mouth, up the dog's rectum. The sooner broke loose and ran. The woman asked the little boy who had taught him that. He said, "That's Old Grim. He can dish it but he can't take it." I said that to tell you to be able to take what you dish out.

Background checks are the best things to do when you are thinking about spending your life with someone. Money is the root of all evil. I haven't seen or heard of anyone who doesn't like money. It isn't the money; it is the things that you can do with it. It makes some people do things they wouldn't usually do. Without money, they do things differently. Some men aren't going to be true. It doesn't make any difference what kind of woman he has. She can own whatever; the sky is the limit for her, and he will still go out and do the wrong thing!

I hope that this book will get to some woman out there who is or who has been having problems with a man. If you follow all of these directions about men, you can't go wrong in choosing your partner for life!